MW01115333

How to Be a
Quality Performer

Five 20-Minute Self-Study Sessions That Build the Skills You Need to Succeed

Featuring

Built-In Learning Reinforcement Tools

Case Studies

Personal Productivity Exercises

Customized Action Plans

Individualized Pre- and Post-Session Skill Assessments

COVER ILLUSTRATION: RANDALL ENOS

CONTENTS

5 CREATING QUALITY SERVICE 67

INTRODUCTION

It sometimes seems as if quality has become the all-important goal in virtually every human endeavor: There is quality control. Quality service. Quality time. Quality product. Quality this, quality that, quality everything. In all businesses, all services, quality is a sort of Holy Grail that everyone constantly strives to attain.

There's no great secret about that. Quality really is that important to success. The secret is that quality itself is so difficult to define. Quality is a ... well, a quality ... that's an abstract. You can't see it, touch it, or feel it. The best we can do is see, touch, or feel an *example* of it and say to ourselves, "Yes, that's a quality coat." Or a quality car. Or even a quality hamburger.

In other words, we can't say what quality is, but we know it when we see it.

Defining quality becomes even more difficult when we move into the area of service and performance. There we do not even have the benefit of a physical product to use as our example of quality. There we are looking at actions, at attitudes, and are forced to decide whether they are quality. Often the only way we can make that determination is by the *reaction* to the actions. If the customers are telling us how pleased they are with our service, we can conclude that we are performing quality customer service.

Because of the importance of quality and the fact that it is an abstraction, it's small wonder that so many books have been devoted to it. In the area of customer service especially, the search for quality has inspired countless volumes filled with approaches, procedures, and techniques for achieving it. That's all well and good, but we believe there is a largely unexplored component to quality that is vital.

And that component is ... you.

The actions that determine a quality performance come from the individual performing them. A quality person performs in a quality manner. Do you have the *personal* attitudes and attributes of quality? What are those attitudes and attributes anyway? Can they be learned, or are they ingrained? Finding and defining the personal characteristics of quality is what *How to Be a Quality Performer* is all about.

As we mentioned, the attributes of quality can be difficult to pin down except by example. It can be even harder when one moves to the *personal* attributes. But we think you'll find it even more interesting. After all, we're talking about you.

This workbook examines what comprises personal quality. It shows you how that translates into your work. And it gives you examples and tests designed to let you practice and perfect the lessons into workable skills you can use to advance your career.

The topics for *How to Be a Quality Performer* are divided into the following five 20-minute work sessions:

Session 1: The Foundations of Quality

Session 2: Meeting the Needs of *All* Your Customers

Session 3: Quality Means Constant Growth

Session 4: The Qualities of Quality

Session 5: Creating Quality Service

To become a quality performer, you must first cultivate the personal characteristics of quality. What are they and how do they work? That's what this workbook will show you.

THE FOUNDATIONS OF QUALITY

Like any sound structure, quality requires a solid foundation. You cannot perform consistently in a quality fashion without developing the basic outlook and attitudes that translate into first-rate work.

The key word here is "consistently." Almost anyone can do a quality job on occasion. But to complete tasks continually in a quality manner requires something more. In short, you have to become a quality worker to turn out quality work consistently.

In this first session, we'll concentrate on those elements that make up a quality-minded personality and show you how these characteristics are applied every day on the job. It starts with attitude — a way of thinking — but that attitude can be learned just like any other skill. With practice, it can become a habit that will boost you and your career to greater heights.

We'll begin Session 1 with a **Pre-Session Skill Level Assessment** to give you an idea of what it's all about and where you stand on the issues of quality.

Next, because quality is indeed a state of mind, we'll show you **Eight Tips to Help You Think Quality.**

How well you can absorb and understand those tips will be tested in **Case Study #1: The New Employee**.

You Gotta Believe: 6 Steps to Self-Motivation will show you ways to increase your own quality-mindedness and give you the opportunity to develop some personalized ideas as well.

The chances of doing a quality job are always better when you have enough time to work on it — and time is always at a premium in the workplace today — so we'll explore that question in the **Quiz: Gaining Control of Your Time.**

Next we'll talk about the importance of personal integrity with a three-in-one problem in **Case Study #2: A Question of Ethics.**

Finally, we'll look at the most important actions you can take to help you become a quality worker in our **Top 5 List of Quality Actions to Remember.**

This session has an **Answers Section** — as do all the sessions in this workbook — which gives replies to some of the questions posed in the exercises.

That is followed by a special section called **Do You Remember?** to see how well you've retained the key points in this session.

Then a **Post-Session Skill Level Assessment** allows you to reevaluate your quality skills, and the session concludes with an **Action Plan** designed to help you define and improve your skills.

Now, turn to the next page to see how solidly you stand on "The Foundations of Quality."

PRE-SESSION SKILL LEVEL ASSESSMENT

Using the following scale, rate your own skills as they relate to the following statements:

WEAK	AVERAGE	STRONG
1–4 points	5–7 points	8–10 points

I believe that what I do is important and makes a difference. _____

I always think in terms of doing a "quality job." _____

I rarely become complacent on the job. _____

I am good at prioritizing tasks. _____

I can focus on the positive even when others are complaining. _____

I have confidence in my day-to-day decision-making capabilities. _____

I maintain a high degree of personal integrity. _____

I can commit fully to all the tasks I perform. _____

I am good at taking personal responsibility for everything I do. _____

I always show enthusiasm for my work. _____

TOTAL RATING _____

WEAK	FAIR	GOOD	STRONG
Under 40	41–55	56–74	75–100

Any score under 55 means there is room for improvement. A score between 56 and 74 means you are doing well but can do better. Any score over 75 means it is just a matter of building on your strengths.

Quality begins in your own mind. It isn't just a result of specific actions; it's also a product of your state of mind. Quality performance comes from quality thinking.

How can you adjust your attitude to improve work practices and results? Consider some of these tips to quality thinking:

1. **There's no such thing as perfection.** A product or service can always be improved. Even when one feature has been optimized, others can be improved. And when every feature of your product or service is sound, you might still be able to add new features. Think of it as a challenge to your imagination.

2. **What's adequate today may not be tomorrow. Change never stops.** Last year's terrific innovation may be obsolete this year. Even if you think you've reached the top in your field or product line, someone will come around tomorrow to redefine what the top is.

3. **Change isn't always good.** Looking for opportunities to make improvements is not the same as looking to change things. Rash changes — even when they seem to be good ideas — sometimes fall flat. Think in terms of the reason for the change.

4. **Satisfaction is trouble.** There's truth to the saying: "That which ceases to grow begins to die." You need to maintain your hunger for improvement just to keep up with the demands of a world that has grown accustomed to constant improvements.

5. **Seek out other people's opinions.** You can't think of everything alone. Other people — even those who aren't experts — may have special ideas or insights of their own. So ask for co-workers' advice and be prepared to act on it.

6. **What seems logical and what works are two different things.** Experience proves that, for every theory that works, 99 others don't. Good ideas deserve to be tested. By the same token, they should be tested before they are accepted.

7. **Consider the possibility that each new idea might create new problems.** Keep in mind that each attempt to improve one item might affect other elements. Watch out for potential repercussions from each new quality improvement you make.

8. **Quality is as quality does.** Don't be presumptuous about quality. Changes for the better are not based on anyone's opinion but on the evidence of absolute improvement and the favorable opinion of buyers.

Try to keep these eight tips in mind and make them a part of your thinking.

CASE STUDY #1:
THE NEW EMPLOYEE

John was eager to make his mark at the company he had joined six weeks earlier. His company was a leading manufacturer of detergents, soaps, and household cleaner. John's department had recently completed an intensive review of the products in their line and was put to the task of developing a list of changes and innovations they would propose to their department manager, who would then make a final presentation to more senior managers. The list included the following:

1. Adding a whitening agent to a successful and popular detergent the company sells.

2. Redesigning the packaging on a household cleanser that is the No. 1 seller in the country.

3. Making the hand soap in their product line — one whose sales are respectable but stagnant — available in a wider variety of sizes and colors.

John was not completely familiar with the company or the products, but he still wanted to have a clear grasp of the pros and cons of each recommendation before the group made their presentation to the boss. He could then back up each idea, anticipate objections, and even suggest new approaches.

Read the eight tips on the previous page again and think about which ones apply to each proposal. There are no right or wrong answers — and more than one of the tips may apply in each case. Write down which of the eight tips might apply to ...

Proposal #1 _____

_____

_____

Proposal #2 _____

_____

_____

Proposal #3 _____

_____

_____

YOU GOTTA BELIEVE:
6 STEPS TO SELF-MOTIVATION

You have to believe in yourself.

Fortunately, most of us have a pretty decent opinion of our own abilities ... most of the time, anyway. But how can you strengthen that belief? Make it more powerful? How can you maintain your belief in the importance of your day-to-day responsibilities?

Here are six methods for doing just that, and each of them can fit easily into your daily routine. Read each method first; then write down a statement you can repeat to yourself mentally to enhance your belief in yourself:

1. **Service counts.** The next time you face a difficult customer, remind yourself that you perform a valuable service for your company. As long as you are talking to the customer — whether in person or on the phone — you *are* the company. All of your co-workers are depending on you.

    Imagine you're with a difficult customer. Write a statement or two that you can say to yourself to strengthen your belief in what you're doing:

    _____

    _____

2. **Satisfy the customer.** A current or potential sale may be riding on it. Instead of thinking about how to "get rid of" the person as quickly as possible, summon up all the skills you have to bring about a satisfactory conclusion.

    Write a motivational statement that you can say to yourself in this situation:

    _____

    _____

3. **Stress quality.** When you've got work backed up, resist the initial impulse to hurry through each task. Each particular task needs your undivided time and attention. If you cannot solve a particular problem yourself, seek help. Don't just pass it on to someone else.

    Write a statement you can use to remind yourself to stress quality when you are overloaded with work:

    _____

    _____

4. **Watch what you say.** When speaking with people outside the company, you never know who is (or could be) a potential customer. Even if you're frustrated over a work-related matter, temper your remarks.

   Write a statement you can use to remind yourself to watch what you say:

   _____

   _____

5. **Think positive.** Accentuate the positive aspects of work rather than joining in when co-workers complain.

   Write a statement you can say to yourself to focus on the positive:

   _____

   _____

6. **Enjoy your successes.** Sure, humility is an asset — but that doesn't mean you cannot luxuriate in some personal satisfaction when you've scored a professional victory. You've earned some self-congratulations, so enjoy them.

   Write down a self-congratulatory statement you can say to yourself for a job well done:

   _____

   _____

Use these personalized motivational statements as often as you can. You'll confirm the belief that what you do is important, worthwhile, and gratifying. It's a belief that can make all the difference.

Some suggested statements for these six steps are in the **Answers Section** on page 14.

<u>Gaining Control of Your Time</u>

Quality is sometimes a function of time. The more time you have for a given project, the easier it is to turn in a quality performance. Unfortunately, there are so many demands made on us today that it's often difficult to get everything done. Do you know what's most important to do now and what can be put off until later? Too many of us react to that issue by doing the easiest or fastest task, which may not be the most important.

Test how you would react by prioritizing the following list of things you need to take care of when you walk into work tomorrow. Number them in order of importance, labeling the most important No. 1, and so on:

Returning calls to customers   _____

Seeing your boss about a problem   _____

Calling a prospective customer   _____

Completing preliminary work for the day (arranging tools, checking schedules, and so on)   _____

Returning a call to a colleague   _____

Starting a two-week project   _____

Checking your voice mail, e-mail, and in-box   _____

Tapping into the office grapevine   _____

Talking with colleagues who dealt with your customers while you were away   _____

Getting briefed about new policies or products   _____

RATE YOUR PRIORITIES: There isn't one best way to handle these 10 tasks, since it would depend on your individual circumstances. However, the following list prescribes a sensible course of action:

1. Seeing your boss about a problem should be your first order of business. The nature of the problem may dictate how you arrange the rest of your tasks.

2. Getting yourself set up for the day.

3. Checking your incoming messages. Chances are your messages will provide you with additional items to add to your list.

4. Returning calls to customers should be in your top five.

5. Calling a prospective customer should come next.

6. Talking with colleagues who dealt with your customers while you were away.

7. Finding out about new policies or procedures.

8. Returning a call to a colleague.

9. Starting a two-week project.

10. Tapping into the office grapevine, where you'll hear about events you missed.

STICKY SITUATIONS

Believing in your own quality requires that you have confidence in the day-to-day decisions you make on the job. Some of the toughest decisions you make involve a choice between right and wrong. There is no separating the fact that a quality performer is an ethical performer.

On the following page is a case study involving three difficult situations. Examine the options available for each and decide what you would do. You are free to develop your own response if none of the listed options seems appropriate to you.

CASE STUDY #2:
A QUESTION OF ETHICS

1. Wayne was sitting at his desk when one of his regular suppliers showed up with a gift for him. The gift was a four-head VCR with on-screen programming.

   "Just wanted to show you how much we appreciate your business," the supplier said to him.

   Wayne figured he could:

   A. Accept the gift and keep it at the office for everyone to use.

   B. Laugh and say, "Throw in a tape and we're in business."

   C. Say, "Thanks but no thanks" and offend the supplier.

   What should Wayne do? What would you do and why?

   _____

   _____

   _____

   _____

2. Martha's boss came into her office and showed her how the answering system could record a phone call using the "memo" button on the machine. She then asked Martha to record a phone conversation without the other person's knowledge.

   Martha realized she could:

   A. Say, "OK, but if we're caught you have to take the responsibility."

   B. Repeat the request and say, "Do I understand that you're asking me to tape a phone conversation without the other person's knowledge?"

   C. Go ahead and do it. After all, she's the boss. She must know what she's doing.

   What should Martha do? What would you do and why?

   _____

   _____

   _____

   _____

3. Shelley accidentally overheard one of her co-workers telling an all-out lie to a customer. The co-worker noticed Shelley nearby and approached her afterward. Shelley realized she could:

    A. Ignore it so she wouldn't be accused of eavesdropping.

    B. Tell the co-worker, "That's a good one. I'll have to use it myself sometime."

    C. Tell a supervisor what she heard.

What should Shelley do? What would you do and why?

_____

_____

_____

_____

Answers are in the **Answers Section** on page 14.

TOP 5 LIST OF QUALITY ACTIONS TO REMEMBER

Following are the top five things you can do to show that you believe in your own quality. They are simple actions that will do wonders for yourself and your career:

1. Take *personal responsibility* for everything you do.

2. Show a *commitment* to everything you do.

3. Show *enthusiasm* for your work.

4. Maintain your personal *integrity*.

5. *Challenge complacency* both personally and in your work.

Memorize these five actions (or at least the key words in italics). We'll be asking about them again later.

YOU GOTTA BELIEVE: 6 STEPS TO SELF-MOTIVATION

The following are suggestions only. The self-motivational statements that will work best for you are those you develop for yourself.

1. Service counts: *If it weren't for me this customer would have walked already.*

2. Satisfy the customer: *I wonder what else I could do to make this customer happy?*

3. Stress quality: *Let me concentrate on this right now, one step at a time.*

4. Watch what you say: *Careful. You can't erase what you say.*

5. Think positive: *Why does everyone always complain? Nothing's perfect, and this job is really pretty good.*

6. Enjoy your successes: *Gee, I really did nail that one, didn't I?*

CASE STUDY #2: A QUESTION OF ETHICS

1. Answer: C. Accepting a notepad or calendar from a supplier who wants to keep your business is one thing. But something as expensive as a VCR? No way. Do not accept the gift.

2. Answer: B. Repeating the request back — with a mild look of shock on your face — lets your boss know that what she's asking is unethical. It gives the boss a chance to change her mind and rescind the request. If she doesn't, you should still refuse and report the matter to a supervisor.

3. Answer: C. Don't say anything to the co-worker. But if you are sure that what you heard was an all-out lie, talk to your supervisor in confidence and tell him or her what you heard.

How many of the **Eight Tips to Help You Think Quality** can you recall from the beginning of this session? Without checking back, write them down here:

1. _____

2. _____

3. _____

4. _____

5. _____

6. _____

7. _____

8. _____

Now go back to page 6 and see which ones you missed. Write them in.

Can you recall the **Top 5 List of Quality Actions to Remember?** List them here.

1. _____

2. _____

3. _____

4. _____

5. _____

POST-SESSION SKILL LEVEL ASSESSMENT

Based on what you've learned in Session 1, rate yourself again on the following statements. When you are finished, compare your total score with the one you earned at the beginning of this session:

WEAK	AVERAGE	STRONG
1–4 points	5–7 points	8–10 points

I believe that what I do is important and makes a difference. _____

I always think in terms of doing a "quality job." _____

I rarely become complacent on the job. _____

I am good at prioritizing tasks. _____

I can focus on the positive even when others are complaining. _____

I have confidence in my day-to-day decision-making capabilities. _____

I maintain a high degree of personal integrity. _____

I can commit fully to all the tasks I perform. _____

I am good at taking personal responsibility for everything I do. _____

I always show enthusiasm for my work. _____

TOTAL RATING _____

WEAK	FAIR	GOOD	STRONG
Under 40	41–55	56–74	75–100

ACTION PLAN

Many of the skills explained in this chapter are interrelated, and building from your strengths is a good place to start improving your overall abilities. But you can't afford to overlook your weaknesses either. List here your three best scores (your strengths) and your three lowest scores (your weaknesses) from the ratings on the previous page:

STRENGTHS

1. _____

2. _____

3. _____

WEAKNESSES

1. _____

2. _____

3. _____

Comparing the two lists, can you see any ways in which you can use your strengths to improve your weaknesses? If so, write them down.

_____

_____

_____

Now reexamine your three biggest weaknesses. It's best to work on them one at a time, so list them in this order: Start with the one you think will be easiest to improve upon, followed by a more difficult one, then the most difficult one.

Next to each, set a timetable for concentrating on them (one week, two weeks, and so on):

WEAKNESSES

1. _____

2. _____

3. _____

TIMETABLE FOR WORKING ON IMPROVEMENT

1. _____

2. _____

3. _____

Using the ideas and information from this session, list at least one technique you can practice to improve each weakness. Also add any ideas of your own.

1. _____

2. _____

3. _____

S U M M A R Y

Quality rises to the top, but it begins at the bottom. And at the very foundation of personal quality is *attitude*. It's what you think, what approach you take toward your personal performance that makes all the difference between doing an acceptable job and a quality one. You must believe in your ability to perform with quality and must learn the skills to do so.

But most important, you have to *want* to be a quality performer.

In our next session, we'll take a look at some ways to provide quality service to customers. We'll also be examining a question that is all too often overlooked: Just who, exactly, are my customers?

The answer may surprise you. That's next in Session 2, "Meeting the Needs of *All* Your Customers."

MEETING THE NEEDS OF *ALL* YOUR CUSTOMERS

<u>I N T R O D U C T I O N</u>

The ultimate aim of any company, or any employee, is to satisfy the customer.

In traditional management, all of the attention is focused on the organization's external customers — the end users of the products or services that organization sells. But quality workers know that there is a second, equally important customer: the internal customer.

In most organizations, different departments and their employees are literally one another's customers. They depend upon one another for information and assistance in order to fulfill that ultimate aim of satisfying the external customer.

In this session, we'll focus first on how you can do a quality job within the company — that is, how to recognize and satisfy your internal customers. We'll show you how to communicate more effectively with these customers and how to do so more efficiently. Then we'll turn our attention to the matter of earning credibility with your external customers in order to serve them more effectively as well.

We'll begin again with our **Pre-Session Skill Level Assessment** to figure out how much you already understand about customer satisfaction and how well you are performing now.

Then we'll proceed with our first exercise, called **Finding — and Defining — Your Internal Customers.** It will show you how to discover who your customers really are and show you that, with a little preparation, you can become more efficient at using your internal customers to help satisfy your external ones.

Four Ways to Become a Super Supplier to Your Internal Customers will give you insights into how to give top-notch "service" to the people within your company.

A Memo on Memos (and Other Written Communications) will show you the secrets to writing memos and business letters clearly, concisely, and quickly. And that's followed by **Case Study #1: The Meeting Memo,** where you'll be given a problem to solve by memo. (If you pick up on the secrets to writing clearly, it'll be easier than you think.)

Three Tips for Making *Them* Believe in You turns our attention to the first step in meeting the needs of external customers: getting *them* to believe in *you*.

Next comes a quiz in which you can not only measure how good you are on the matter of credibility with customers but also learn when and how your credibility comes into question. It's called **Do Customers Question Your Credibility?**

Finally, we'll have another scenario for you to look at in **Case Study #2: The Late Call.**

As in all the sessions, there is an **Answers Section** at the end so you can see how well you did. And there's our **Do You Remember?** section to help you keep some of the major points in mind.

The **Post-Session Skill Level Assessment** can show you how much progress you've made just by working through this session, and the **Action Plan** will give you a method for continuing your personal growth in these areas.

Now turn to the next page for "Meeting the Needs of *All* Your Customers."

Using the following scale, rate your own skills as they relate to the following statements:

WEAK	AVERAGE	STRONG
1–4 points	5–7 points	8–10 points

I understand why co-workers are customers too. _____

I have a strong working knowledge of all departments within the company. _____

I know the importance of both internal and external customers. _____

I am good at communicating with others within the company. _____

I can write clear and concise memos and business letters. _____

I know whom to contact within the organization for specific problems. _____

I recognize when a customer is challenging my credibility. _____

I am a team player, willing to help others out. _____

I know when to make a promise to a customer. _____

I know when not to make a promise to a customer; I don't bow to pressure. _____

TOTAL RATING _____

WEAK	FAIR	GOOD	STRONG
Under 40	41–55	56–74	75–100

Any score under 55 means there is room for improvement. A score between 56 and 74 means you are doing well but can do better. Any score over 75 means it is just a matter of building on your strengths.

FINDING — AND DEFINING — YOUR INTERNAL CUSTOMERS

Of all of the customers you deal with, which one is the single most important one for you to keep satisfied? The answer should be easy. And if it takes you more than a second to come up with it, it's time for you to broaden your definition of "customers."

The answer: your boss.

You don't think of your boss as your customer? Think again. He or she is counting on you to provide certain services. So are many other people in your company. And eventually, of course, so are your external customers — those people who buy your product or service.

Thinking in terms of being a supplier to internal as well as external customers is a key step in becoming a quality worker. A company cannot satisfy its external customers until it can satisfy its internal needs. And the same is true for you.

Here's an example: By understanding your particular organization, its people, and all of its services, you will know whom to contact if a customer, business associate, or you need something that is handled by another department.

To accomplish this more easily, do the exercise on the following page.

Under the heading "Department," list all of your company's departments. Then list the product or service that department is responsible for. Finally, list the person — or the "contact" — whom you can call for help in that area. Where possible, list more than one contact for each department.

After you've finished, make a copy of the list and keep it on hand.

Not only will you have a better understanding of where your job fits into the big picture, but you'll also be able to identify how you can help your co-workers.

Department	Product/Service	Contact
_____	_____	_____
	(Second contact)	_____
_____	_____	_____
	(Second contact)	_____
_____	_____	_____
	(Second contact)	_____
_____	_____	_____
	(Second contact)	_____
_____	_____	_____
	(Second contact)	_____
_____	_____	_____
	(Second contact)	_____
_____	_____	_____
	(Second contact)	_____
_____	_____	_____
	(Second contact)	_____
_____	_____	_____
	(Second contact)	_____
_____	_____	_____
	(Second contact)	_____
_____	_____	_____
	(Second contact)	_____
_____	_____	_____
	(Second contact)	_____
_____	_____	_____
	(Second contact)	_____

FOUR WAYS TO BECOME A SUPER SUPPLIER TO YOUR INTERNAL CUSTOMERS

Here are four ways to perform with quality for your internal customers:

1. **Respond to their requests.** When a co-worker calls, get back to him or her quickly. Another employee may need your expertise to serve a client. You'll encourage co-workers to return your calls quickly if that's the treatment they get from you.

2. **Be a team player.** If you find a handy tip for performing a task, let others know about it. Share information about new products and services.

3. **Lend a helping hand.** Is that phone at the next desk ringing? Answer it. Does a co-worker need files you can locate? Retrieve them. Is a colleague trying to serve three customers simultaneously while two more wait? Help out.

4. **Communicate.** Don't depend on managers to relay all the information you need. Take it upon yourself to keep the flow of communications going between work areas and departments. Get to know each other and understand each other's needs. Isn't that what makes service succeed?

Memorize these four ways to be a super supplier to your internal customers.

A MEMO ON MEMOS (AND OTHER WRITTEN COMMUNICATIONS)

Much has been written about written communications. Internal memos and letters to customers sometimes read like texts on astrophysics or (worse) legal documents.

Whether you're writing to one of your co-workers (an internal customer) or to someone outside (external customer), the first rule is to keep it plain and simple. Long words and heavy jargon don't make you look more intelligent. They simply confuse.

You don't have to be a first-rate writer to compose quality communications. All you need is a little organizational thinking. Before you begin to write, make a few notes for yourself along the following lines, using a variation of the old journalistic formula.

To compose a quality memo or business letter, ask yourself:

1. **Why?** What is the specific reason for your letter? To inform someone of something? To ask someone to do something? To respond to a communication you received? Keep the purpose for your letter clearly in mind.

2. **Who?** Think for a moment about who will be reading your memo. A co-worker? A superior? An angry customer? Put yourself in their shoes and imagine their probable reactions before you start writing. This can save you a great deal of time and trouble and make your communication stronger at the same time. To give just one example, suppose you are writing a co-worker a memo regarding a project you are both involved in. There's no need to spend time explaining the background. Your reader will already be familiar with it.

3. **What?** What is the most important point you want to convey? That a meeting is scheduled for 10 A.M.? Or that a decision will be made at that meeting and certain materials will be needed for it? Try to determine the single most important point.

4. **When?** This one is trickier and will depend upon the nature of your written communication. But "when" you should send off the memo or letter could be crucial to how it is received. If it's going to arrive too late for anyone to act on it, for instance, you are better off not sending it. Similarly, if the letter is premature, it may be forgotten by the time the recipient can act on it. Before you send it off, remember, timing is everything.

C A S E   S T U D Y   # 1 :
T H E   M E E T I N G   M E M O

John's boss has just informed him of an interdepartmental meeting he wants to hold next Thursday at 2 P.M. He wants John to write a memo to the other department heads informing them of it. He also wants John to recap his department's position on a new product, which will be the subject of the meeting.

This meeting will be a follow-up to the one held the day before at which three options were discussed for action on a new product. The three options were: (1) to go ahead with the new product introduction; (2) to delay the introduction for a few months while additional research is conducted, or (3) to put the new product introduction on indefinite hold.

A final decision is to be made at this meeting.

John was involved in the previous meeting and is also on the team that developed the new product. Although he is eager to see the new product introduced, he knows that if that happens and the product is flawed, his job may well be on the line.

What does John do? What would you do?

Write the memo John's boss requested, keeping it as brief as possible. See if you can do it in no more than two paragraphs. If you can keep it to one paragraph, better yet.

_____

_____

_____

_____

_____

_____

_____

A sample memo is in the **Answers Section** on page 30.

THREE TIPS FOR MAKING *THEM* BELIEVE IN YOU

In Session 1 we showed you how important it is to believe in your own quality. Unfortunately, that inner belief doesn't automatically translate into a customer (internal or external) believing in your quality, too. Your credibility with a customer is only as good as your word.

Here are three tips for gaining and maintaining credibility and making customers believe in you:

1. **Know what is impossible.** Promises can get you in trouble if you don't know all the facts. If you aren't sure, find out before you commit yourself.

2. **Don't bow to pressure.** When a customer, co-worker, or boss is in a hurry, you may not have time to think of all the consequences. But don't just tell people what they want to hear. The truth is better than broken promises.

3. **Keep your promises.** If you do give your word, you'd better follow through. You'll gain a reputation as someone to be trusted.

Don't forget these three tips. Memorize them now.

Do Customers Question Your Credibility?

The three basic ways to win credibility are to earn it, to have it given to you by a referral, and to have it reflected on you through your product's or company's reputation. The first step in maintaining credibility is to know when customers are testing it. Assume that a customer makes each of the following statements. Then ask yourself in each case: "Is this a test of my credibility?" Write **YES** or **NO** after each question:

	YES	NO
1. "I've never heard of you or your company. What can you tell me about your outfit?"	_____	_____
2. "Are you sure you can get this for me by the 15th? A lot depends on it getting here by then."	_____	_____
3. "What can you tell me about your competitors?"	_____	_____
4. "My banker tells me you're just starting out. Why should I trust my business to a novice?"	_____	_____
5. "Your company has a good reputation, but I don't know much about your product line. What can you tell me?"	_____	_____
6. "Would you like to know what your competition said about this same job? I've got the information right here."	_____	_____

SCORING:

1. NO. Since the person hasn't heard of you or your company — and mentions no referral — it's safe to assume that any credibility has yet to be established. And you can't lose what you don't have.

2. YES. The customer is testing your credibility. A lot is riding on what you've already told the person. This might be the ideal time to use the phone and call the office or factory to guarantee the delivery.

3. YES. The customer is using a roundabout way to test you. The correct response is not to knock your competitors. Doing so tells people you don't have enough faith in your company and its products to let them stand on their own.

4. YES. This person already has a referral concerning you, so he or she is obviously interested. Your challenge is to prove you're not a novice.

5. **YES.** You're credible when you know about your product line — no matter what your job title is. The best response here might be: "Could you be more specific so that I won't cover material you're already familiar with?"

6. **NO.** This is a test of your integrity. Make it clear that you stand behind what your company stated, no matter what the competition had to say.

C A S E   S T U D Y   # 2 :
T H E   L A T E   C A L L

Laura took the call shortly before 5 P.M., a few minutes before the office closed for the day. The customer wanted to place an order and insisted that it be delivered the next morning. Although Laura was fairly new on the job, she knew that — while her company ordinarily did not offer overnight delivery — it was possible under certain conditions and for an extra fee.

But she was going to need an approval from the proper person in the proper department within the company, and she had no idea who that was. The customer was demanding an immediate answer.

What should Laura say or do? What would you do? What would you not do?

_____

_____

_____

_____

_____

_____

What could Laura do to be prepared for a similar situation in the future?

_____

_____

_____

_____

CASE STUDY #1:
THE MEETING MEMO

(John's memo)

RE: New Product Introduction

At 2 P.M. on Thursday we will meet again in Conference Room B to make a final decision on the new product introduction we discussed yesterday. Our department's opinion is that the new product is ready to be introduced at this time, although we share some of the concerns voiced yesterday and are willing to pursue one of the other options if a convincing case can be made for doing so. Therefore, please bring all relevant materials and reports to the meeting.

(John does not bother to mention the three options specifically because he knows that everyone who was in yesterday's meeting will be familiar with them.)

DO YOU REMEMBER?

Can you recall the **Four Ways to Become a Super Supplier to Your Internal Customers** listed in this session? Write them here:

1._____

2._____

3._____

4._____

Write the **Three Tips for Making *Them* Believe in You**

1._____

2._____

3._____

Based on what you've learned in Session 2, rate yourself again on the following statements. When you are finished, compare your total score with the one you earned at the beginning of this session.

WEAK	AVERAGE	STRONG
1–4 points	5–7 points	8–10 points

I understand why co-workers are customers too. _____

I have a strong working knowledge of all departments within the company. _____

I know the importance of both internal and external customers. _____

I am good at communicating with others within the company. _____

I can write clear and concise memos and business letters. _____

I know whom to contact within the organization for specific problems. _____

I recognize when a customer is challenging my credibility. _____

I am a team player, willing to help others out. _____

I know when to make a promise to a customer. _____

I know when not to make a promise to a customer; I don't bow to pressure. _____

TOTAL RATING _____

WEAK	FAIR	GOOD	STRONG
Under 40	41–55	56–74	75–100

A C T I O N   P L A N

Many of the skills explained in this chapter are interrelated, and building from your strengths is a good place to start improving your overall abilities. But you can't afford to overlook your weaknesses either. List your three best scores (your strengths) and your three lowest scores (your weaknesses) from the ratings on the previous page.

STRENGTHS

1. _____

2. _____

3. _____

WEAKNESSES

1. _____

2. _____

3. _____

Comparing the two lists, can you see any ways in which you can use your strengths to improve your weaknesses? If so, write them down.

_____

_____

_____

Now examine your three biggest weaknesses. It's best to work on them one at a time, so list them in this order: Start with the one you think will be easiest to improve upon, followed by a more difficult one, then the most difficult one.

Next to each, set a timetable for concentrating on them (one week, two weeks, and so on):

WEAKNESSES

1. _____

2. _____

3. _____

TIMETABLE FOR WORKING ON IMPROVEMENT

1. _____

2. _____

3. _____

Using the ideas and information from this session, list at least one technique you can practice to improve each weakness. Also add any ideas of your own:

1. _____

2. _____

3. _____

S U M M A R Y

Satisfying the customer is the single most basic requirement of any business professional. It is so basic — a given, in fact — that we barely stop to think about it. It's practically an inbred instinct.

But we also rarely stop to think and recognize that our customers are internal as well as external. (Indeed, in some jobs the only customers are internal ones.) Keeping them satisfied with your performance is crucial to an overall quality performance and to your career.

Developing a sharp awareness of that reality is the first step to success. Top-level communication skills and personal credibility are two keys to ensuring it; and they are keys that are vital to pleasing *all* of your customers as well.

In Session 3, "Quality Means Constant Growth," we're going to look at another aspect of quality performance: the need for continual improvement.

QUALITY MEANS CONSTANT GROWTH

I N T R O D U C T I O N

A true quality performer is one who is "getting better all the time." Doing the same job well — and doing it consistently well — is only the beginning. To reach your maximum potential, you have to grow. You have to seek out new challenges and look for new opportunities.

It can be a little unsettling at times. When you feel you've mastered your specific work, when you know you're handling it superbly, the risks of taking on something you know little or nothing about can seem like jumping off into the unknown. The chances for failure are suddenly higher, and the tendency is often to stick with the tried and true. But that path can lead to stagnation, both on the personal and professional level.

Quality means improvement, and improvement is a constant process.

In this session, we'll show you how to make personal growth a constant in your career. We'll start with our **Pre-Session Skill Level Assessment** to see if you recognize some of the abilities you'll need and to check just how well you think you're doing right now.

Then we'll offer some solutions to a problem many people face on the job — the stagnation that can occur when you start to feel bored with your job or even your career. This first exercise is called **Four Positive Steps Toward "Breaking Out."**

Next we'll examine ways to expand your work horizons and give you some tips for handling those new challenges in **New Projects Lead to Personal Growth.**

Our **Case Study #1: Uncharted Waters** will give you the chance to put some of those tips into practice and help you refine and adapt the ideas to your own needs. That will be followed by an instructive test, our **Quiz: Look Before You Leap into New Projects.**

Personal and professional growth isn't just about expanding. It's also about minimizing certain things. Such as mistakes. That's the topic of the exercise **Can You Ever Be Error-Free?**

Case Study #2: Well-Laid Plans will test your abilities to plan a new project before it starts to help ensure its successful conclusion. Here's a hint: You might want to "look before you leap" before you answer this one.

The next exercise, **Quiz: The Road Less Traveled Leads to Rewarding Destinations**, will not only test your innovative abilities but also give you ideas for developing that highly prized skill of creative thinking.

As always, we'll have our **Answers Section** and **Do You Remember?** quiz and conclude with the **Post-Session Skill Level Assessment** and **Action Plan**.

By that time you should be well prepared to take on any new challenges that come your way.

Using the following scale, rate your own skills as they relate to the following statements.

WEAK	AVERAGE	STRONG
1–4 points	5–7 points	8–10 points

I realize that personal growth requires new challenges. _____

I always try to learn new job skills. _____

I am good at working within a team. _____

I can organize new tasks I have never attempted before. _____

I am willing to take on new or special projects. _____

I am good at setting personal goals. _____

I build and maintain working relationships throughout the company. _____

I recognize error-prone situations — times when I'm most likely to make mistakes. _____

I know how to minimize mistakes and errors. _____

I can focus on one thing at a time when I am very busy. _____

TOTAL RATING _____

WEAK	FAIR	GOOD	STRONG
Under 40	41–55	56–74	75–100

Any score under 55 means there is room for improvement. A score between 56 and 74 means you are doing well but can do better. Any score over 75 means it is just a matter of building on your strengths.

FOUR POSITIVE STEPS
TOWARD "BREAKING OUT"

Everyone hits those times when they begin to get a little bored with their job, and when that happens your performance — and your promotion possibilities — are bound to suffer.

Here are four positive steps you can take to break out of that rut:

1. **Learn a new job skill.** Mastering a new computer skill or developing expertise in a particular area can do wonders for your outlook. Broaden your horizons by acquiring new knowledge.

2. **Expand your network.** Establishing productive relationships with people both inside and outside your organization can give your career new life. Learn what you can from others, and give of your own experience as well.

3. **Set goals for yourself.** Give yourself something to work for and reward yourself when you achieve it. If you can't think of any goals, then it's your mind that's stuck in a rut — not your job.

4. **Ask for more responsibility.** Shake up your routine by throwing some new duties into the mix. You'll show that you're a team player and earn allies by helping your peers.

Try to memorize these four steps.

Now think about your own job and, for each of the four steps, write down one positive step you could take. Even if you're not bored with your job, putting one or more of these steps into practice can only help your career.

1. _____

2. _____

3. _____

4. _____

One pathway to improving your quality performance is to take on new projects. This is an excellent step toward personal growth for it allows you to explore new ground and learn new skills. Like any new endeavor, however, it can at first seem a bit overwhelming. Here are some guidelines for successfully handling a new project.

Suppose that you and several co-workers from different areas of the company have been put together on a special projects team. Your assignment is to look for ways to improve productivity without increasing costs. The goal is clear enough, if somewhat broad, but just the same you don't know what to do.

Here are some suggestions:

1. At your next team meeting, suggest that you and your co-workers focus on one improvement at a time. Whether it's decreasing waste, improving safety, building customer relations, or increasing workflow efficiency, brainstorm with team members on how to improve one idea at a time.

2. Suggest that each team member develop at least one suggestion for improvement, a means of implementing that improvement, and the possible results. When it comes to an idea you'll work on, make sure your suggestion is concrete and attainable.

3. When suggestions are proposed, discuss each one as a team. Here are some key questions to ask to help determine the validity of the suggestion:

   A. How much will it cost to make that change?

   B. How can I help implement that suggestion in my area?

   C. What will the organization save as a result of this improvement?

   D. What will the effect of the change be? (Are there any negative consequences or downsides to effecting the change?)

4. Be a team player when adopting the suggestions. You may not completely agree with the solutions, but each member of the team must be committed to what works best for the whole team if it's going to be successful.

Of course, a new project can be a solo effort, too. If that's the case, simply apply the first three guidelines to yourself. And don't hesitate to bounce your ideas off other co-workers for additional thoughts and insights.

C A S E   S T U D Y   # 1 :
U N C H A R T E D   W A T E R S

Sheila's boss called her into his office and asked her if she would be part of a special task force. This would be a company-wide initiative which would involve employees from several different departments at various levels. But regardless of their position, each member of this team would have an opportunity for input and feedback. Sheila knew this could help her get that promotion she wanted and agreed to participate.

The project involved new business. The goal of the project was twofold: (1) to devise the outlines of presentations for acquiring new business that would minimize the day-to-day disruption of ordinary business and (2) to develop suggestions for reducing the out-of-pocket expense to the company without compromising competitiveness in future new business presentations.

Sheila had never been a part of anything remotely like this and immediately realized that she was sailing into uncharted waters. What should Sheila do? What would you do?

Use suggestions 1 and 2 on the previous page as a rough guideline for how to proceed. What are some key questions to ask yourself to determine the validity of your ideas?

Look Before You Leap into New Projects

Your ability to carry out your tasks properly is a crucial element of your personal quality. Your chances for exciting, stimulating, and challenging new assignments and your opportunities for promotion largely depend on your ability to perform delegated tasks satisfactorily. Now begin taking the necessary steps to launch your next new project successfully. This quiz can set you on the right track. Write **YES** or **NO** after each question; then score yourself.

1. Before accepting an assignment, do you make sure you understand completely what you are supposed to do? _____

2. Are the deadlines clear? _____

3. Is it clear how much responsibility and authority you have in the project? _____

4. Do you know which tasks you can perform on your own without reporting back to your boss? _____

5 Do you let your boss know if a new assignment makes it difficult for you to do your other jobs? _____

6. Do you make suggestions to set priorities on how much time you will allow the project? _____

7. Do you get the information and background material you need to do the job properly? _____

8. Do you try to imagine all the problems and obstacles that could arise while you are doing the job — and then plan accordingly? _____

9. Is it clear who makes decisions when your boss is not available? _____

10. If a problem arises that you can't handle, do you talk to your boss about the situation? _____

HOW DID YOU SCORE? If you answered nine or 10 questions **YES**, you are doing an excellent job of getting new projects off to the right start. Keep that up, and you'll significantly lower the possibility for errors and mistakes. If you scored any lower, take the corrective action explained in the questions you missed the next time you accept a project, and you'll be well on your way to performing your tasks more effectively.

Not if you're human. It's difficult to find a truer maxim than the one that says "everyone makes mistakes."

Does that mean you should just accept this fact of life and move on from there?

Of course not. Improving your quality performance doesn't just mean growth. It means shrinking, too ... that is, constantly reducing the errors you make on the job until they are few and very far between.

Many, if not most, of the errors we make at work fall into a pattern. That pattern doesn't necessarily have to do with the work or the task itself, but rather with the *conditions under which we attempt to perform it.* When you are tired or worn out, for example, the chances of making a mistake are considerably higher than if you are fresh and alert.

To find out what patterns allow errors to creep into your work, complete the following exercise.

First, think of a mistake you have made at work. Then write down why you think it happened.

_____

Have you ever made other mistakes because of the same reason? Do you see a pattern there?

_____

Recognizing the reasons why you made an error — the conditions under which that error happened — can help you eliminate your mistakes by changing, or even simply becoming more aware of, those conditions.

Think of working situations or conditions that can make you prone to mistakes. List as many as you can.

Error-Prone Situations

1. _____

2. _____

3. _____

4. _____

5. _____

Now try to think of some simple solutions to change those conditions. For example: Error-prone situation #1: Exhausted at work. Solution #1: Take a break or, if possible, put off intensive tasks until the next morning.

Solutions

1. _____

2. _____

3. _____

4. _____

5. _____

Some common error-prone situations and suggestions for solving them are in the **Answers Section** on page 46.

CASE STUDY #2:
WELL-LAID PLANS

Paul was certainly glad not to be in Mary's shoes. Mary was Paul's already overworked boss who had just accepted an assignment to head a task force that would find and develop cost-cutting procedures for their company. Paul did wonder to himself, though, what he would do in Mary's place because, who knew, maybe someday he'd be there.

Paul considered the negatives. The time frame for completing the project was extremely short; if Mary recommended a course of action that didn't pan out, she would be blamed; and a similar project had been carried out a year ago and had been a failure. It was a very difficult assignment.

On the positive side, the assignment could be a big boost to Mary's career — assuming a moderate level of success. Paul even had a few ideas himself that he thought he would suggest to Mary. After all, his career could use a little boost, too.

Paul knew the key to handling this project was to lay out some plans.

What would Paul do if he was in Mary's situation? What would he ask for to run the project smoothly? What would you do? Write down your ideas and plans in the following space:

_____

_____

_____

_____

_____

_____

_____

_____

Road Less Traveled Leads to Rewarding Destinations

Innovative, creative thinking is a key component of continuous improvement. One of the best-kept secrets about creative thinking is that it does not come naturally for everyone. Yet many of the most creative people *learned how* to think that way. They've learned that certain actions and behaviors will help trick their minds into new ways of thinking. It's a skill we can all develop to one degree or another. See how successful you are at reengineering your thinking. Write **YES** or **NO** after each question, then score yourself:

1. Do you take the initiative to work on projects with someone with whom you've never worked before? _____

2. Have you ever volunteered for a task that "scares" you because you thought it was beyond you or too risky or challenging? _____

3. Have you tried learning a completely new skill? _____

4. Do you take part in brainstorming sessions where the floor is open to even the most "far out" solution to a problem? _____

5. Do you vary your schedule or take a different route to work to help you start your day with a fresh new perspective? _____

6. Do you listen to the ideas and opinions of co-workers and appreciate the depth of their knowledge? _____

7. Are you always on the lookout for ways to cut costs and reduce errors? _____

8. Do you prioritize your tasks to focus on the most urgent but still leave time to pursue new ideas? _____

9. Do you use your weekends and vacation times as periods to recharge your batteries and gain a fresh perspective on how you do things? _____

10. Do you constantly reevaluate your strategies to ensure that you never stray too far off track? _____

YOUR SCORE: You should have answered each question **YES**. That would indicate you are already very successful at getting into a more creative mind-set. Seven or eight is average. Look at those questions you responded **NO** to, and incorporate the behavior into your daily routine. You'll see a rise in your innovative thinking.

CAN YOU EVER BE ERROR-FREE?

Some common error-prone situations include the following:

1. You are in a rush to finish.

2. You are working on more than one task at a time.

3. You are unfamiliar with the task; it is a new experience.

4. You are nervous about the boss' or client's reaction.

5. You are ill.

Solutions to these situations include the following:

1. Force yourself to slow down; ask for more time to complete the task.

2. Focus your main attention on one task until it is completed; if that is impossible, schedule specific blocks of time to work on individual projects.

3. Ask for help. And not just once, but each time you have a question. If you have never done a particular type of task before, no one can fault you for being unfamiliar with it. They can fault you if you do not seek to learn what you don't know.

4. Work toward developing at least a passing relationship with your boss or client. Try to get to know them a little on a personal level. Familiarity breeds confidence.

5. Call in sick and stay home. Struggling into work despite an illness doesn't help anyone if it results in mistakes and errors.

DO YOU REMEMBER?

Write as many of the **Four Positive Steps Toward "Breaking Out"** as you can remember.

1. _____

2. _____

3. _____

4. _____

Based on what you've learned in Session 3, rate yourself again on the following statements. When you are finished, compare your total score with the one you earned at the beginning of this session:

WEAK	AVERAGE	STRONG
1–4 points	5–7 points	8–10 points

I realize that personal growth requires new challenges. _____

I always try to learn new job skills. _____

I am good at working within a team. _____

I can organize new tasks I have never attempted before. _____

I am willing to take on new or special projects. _____

I am good at setting personal goals. _____

I build and maintain working relationships throughout the company. _____

I recognize error-prone situations — times when I'm most likely to make mistakes. _____

I know how to minimize mistakes and errors. _____

I can focus on one thing at a time when I am very busy. _____

TOTAL RATING _____

WEAK	FAIR	GOOD	STRONG
Under 40	41–55	56–74	75–100

A C T I O N   P L A N

Many of the skills explained in this chapter are interrelated, and building from your strengths is a good place to start improving your overall abilities. But you can't afford to overlook your weaknesses either. List your three best scores (your strengths) and your three lowest scores (your weaknesses) from the ratings on the previous page:

STRENGTHS	WEAKNESSES
1. _____	1. _____
2. _____	2. _____
3. _____	3. _____

Comparing the two lists, can you see any ways in which you can use your strengths to improve your weaknesses? If so, write them down.

_____

_____

_____

Now reexamine your three biggest weaknesses. It's best to work on them one at a time, so list them in this order: Start with the one you think will be easiest to improve upon, followed by a more difficult one, then the most difficult one.

Next to each, set a timetable for concentrating on them (one week, two weeks, and so on):

WEAKNESSES	TIMETABLE FOR WORKING ON IMPROVEMENT
1. _____	1. _____
2. _____	2. _____
3. _____	3. _____

Using the ideas and information from this session, list at least one technique you can practice to improve each weakness. Also add any ideas of your own.

1. _____

2. _____

3. _____

S U M M A R Y

You may be a quality performer today, but that's no guarantee that you will be tomorrow. Quality *does* demand constant growth. You have to be constantly adding to your professional repertoire, developing new skills, and learning new techniques. Time won't stand still, and neither should you.

Accepting new projects and learning how to think creatively are two methods for ensuring that you continue to grow as a professional. Finding new ways to minimize errors is another. Overall, a personal strategy that seeks out and takes on new challenges is the key to constant growth.

In Session 4, "The Qualities of Quality," we're going to examine just what that elusive term *quality* is. We'll look at what it is composed of, at some of the many components that combine to create it.

THE QUALITIES OF QUALITY

If you were buying a fine luxury car or an expensively made suit, it would be fairly easy to see in detail the many components that made it a top-quality item. The same could be said for any top-of-the-line product. The qualities that add up to quality are often visible and discernible.

With quality service, it can be a little more difficult to figure out what elements constitute quality because it involves quality in action. Still, there are procedures and tangible actions that, when taken together, spell out quality. And for truly outstanding quality service, there is often positive feedback that follows in its wake.

But what about a breakdown of personal quality? How can you distinguish between a true quality performer and one who is just sliding by? What, after all, *is* personal quality? What separate elements or characteristics — what qualities — add up to a quality performer?

That's the question we'll answer in Session 4.

We'll begin again with the **Pre-Session Skill Level Assessment** to see where you stand on some of the qualities of quality. Then we'll give you a chance to define those qualities yourself in our first exercise, **What Is Quality Made Of?**

The 3 Guiding Principles of Personal Quality will show you some of the most important of those qualities of quality.

In **Case Study #1: Of Responses and Responsibility**, you'll be given the opportunity to determine what course of action you would take in a difficult situation based upon one of those key qualities.

Our next feature is a quiz called **How Quality-Conscious Are You?** Here's your chance to find out how you measure up in terms of quality awareness and attitude.

Possessing all the good qualities you do won't mean too much, however, if you never translate them into quality actions. We'll give you a few helpful hints on how to do just that in **Four Quick Tips for Showing Your Qualities**.

Our next item, **Qualities in Action**, expands upon those tips. It is an exercise that will help you see the relationship between attitude and action, and will give you a little practice in honing your skills.

Case Study #2: A Quality Proposal puts you in the middle of a ticklish dilemma in which you'll examine your own quality-related skills and try to decide what's the best way to proceed in what just may be a no-win situation.

You won't be too busy with our **Answers Section** in this session because we're holding back more replies than usual. As you'll see, the reason is that an all-inclusive list of qualities that make up quality can indeed be difficult to determine on the personal level.

Our **Do You Remember?** section comes next and is followed by the **Post-Session Skill Level Assessment** and **Action Plan** which conclude the session.

To start on Session 4, "The Qualities of Quality," go to the next page now.

PRE-SESSION SKILL LEVEL ASSESSMENT

Using the following scale, rate your own skills as they relate to the following statements.

WEAK	AVERAGE	STRONG
1–4 points	5–7 points	8–10 points

I have an ongoing commitment to always do quality work. _____

I am good at paying attention to the everyday mundane tasks. _____

I always take responsibility for whatever I do. _____

I can perform consistently at a high level. _____

I am conscious of the need for quality within the company. _____

I have a thorough knowledge of company products and services. _____

I believe in being accountable for whatever I do, including mistakes. _____

I have confidence in my own abilities. _____

I communicate clearly; I am rarely misunderstood or asked to reexplain. _____

I am personable; co-workers and clients like to work with me. _____

TOTAL RATING _____

WEAK	FAIR	GOOD	STRONG
Under 40	41–55	56–74	75–100

Any score under 55 means there is room for improvement. A score between 56 and 74 means you are doing well but can do better. Any score over 75 means it is just a matter of building on your strengths.

WHAT IS QUALITY MADE OF?

Quality workers do quality work. But what qualities do quality workers possess? What traits do they have that set them apart from and above ordinary workers?

It's all but impossible to make a comprehensive, all-inclusive list. Most of us will possess some "quality qualities" to a strong degree and be a little short on others. But to bring ourselves to the level of a true, top-notch quality performer, we need to build up as many of those qualities as possible.

What qualities are they? Let's see what you think. Complete the following exercise as best you can.

Suppose you are interviewing to hire a person who will be your assistant or subordinate. What personal qualities would you want in this person? List them here.

1. _____

2. _____

3. _____

4. _____

5. _____

6. _____

7. _____

8. _____

You will find a list of qualities in the **Answers Section** on page 62. But before you check them out, take another look at your list. How many of the qualities you wrote down are qualities that *you* possess to a significant degree?

THE 3 GUIDING PRINCIPLES
OF PERSONAL QUALITY

Although there are many traits and skills that go into the making of a quality performer, perhaps three are the most crucial. Think of them as the guiding principles of personal quality and work to make certain they are a part of your work character:

1. **Responsibility.** Be responsible for your work and for yourself. This means far more than simply taking responsibility for any tasks assigned to you or for any mistakes you might make. It means being responsible for all of your actions on the job. It means taking the attitude that you are responsible for your own, your team's, and your company's success. It means taking responsibility for solving those small problems that might have suddenly arisen or slipped through the cracks — even when they are not your assigned tasks.

2. **Consistency.** Personal quality performance is defined in the long run. But it is accomplished on a day-to-day level. Doing a bang-up job on that vital assignment is important. But so is the work you turn out on the more mundane, everyday chores. It is the consistent quality of your work, over time, that will make you a quality performer.

3. **Commitment.** A commitment to quality means that you are always conscious of quality and that your personal standards will accept no less in your own work. Being "quality-conscious" is something that can be learned fairly simply (we'll show you how a little later in this session); making the commitment to quality is somewhat more difficult. Everyone experiences those nagging, annoying little tasks that you want to just get done and over with as quickly as possible. Commitment to quality requires that you perform all of your tasks — even the smallest ones — to the best of your abilities.

Memorize these three guiding principles. We'll be asking about them again later.

Art's team leader had just handed him a plum assignment. Their team wanted to propose some improvement recommendations to the CEO of the company and Richard, the team leader, had selected Art to draft the proposal. "You always do quality work, Art. That's why I picked you," Richard said. "I want the same type of performance on this one."

Richard went on to explain that Art would need additional input from the Senior Vice President of Marketing to put the proposal together. Art had never dealt directly with senior management before; he was used to dealing with the departmental managers in marketing.

Richard asked when Art could have the proposal finished. "I'll have it for you next week," Art replied.

Art began working on it but experienced some delay in getting additional input that he needed from the marketing vice president. It was the end of the week before he had all the information. Late Monday, Richard asked Art for the completed proposal. Art told him it wasn't finished. Richard was upset because he had promised the CEO the proposal for Tuesday. "You said it would be ready this week," Richard said. "I told the CEO he would have it tomorrow."

Obviously, there was a miscommunication between Art and Richard. What should Art say? What would you say? What should Art suggest as a course of action? What would you suggest? And what about the delay Art experienced in getting the material from the marketing VP? There are no right or wrong answers, but keep in mind the principles of responsibility, consistency, and commitment explained on the previous page as you write down your ideas.

_____

_____

_____

_____

_____

_____

_____

How Quality-Conscious Are You?

It's easy to say you're always conscious of quality. But sometimes we're not as aware of quality as we'd like to think we are. How about you? Is quality a quality that's foremost on your mind? Take this test and find out. Mark the following statements **TRUE** or **FALSE** and then check your score:

1. When it comes to quality, there's always room for improvement.   _____

2. Nobody can be aware of quality needs all of the time.   _____

3. Customers pay little attention to quality.   _____

4. A quality program must mesh with the organization's goals and profit plans.   _____

5. Quality means conformance to standards.   _____

6. Quality should operate in all parts of a business.   _____

7. Personal quality standards and business quality standards have little in common.   _____

8. Quality requires commitment.   _____

9. Quality relates to the process as much as to the goal.   _____

10. People who talk about quality are mostly idealists.   _____

ANSWERS: (1) **TRUE**; (2) **FALSE**. Quality doesn't evolve by itself. It requires the constant attention of everyone in the organization; (3) **FALSE**. Customers today are sophisticated and demanding. They pay as much attention to quality as to price; (4), (5), and (6), **TRUE**; (7) **FALSE**. Personal and business quality standards are inseparable. People with high personal standards will be the ones to lead business quality programs. (8) and (9), **TRUE**; (10) **FALSE**. People who talk about quality are realists. The only way to compete successfully today is to improve quality continually.

The passing grade for the test is 10. If you missed just one answer, you are failing in at least one key area. Concentrate on those statements that you evaluated incorrectly and try to turn your attitude around.

FOUR QUICK TIPS FOR SHOWING YOUR QUALITIES

Sometimes it's the little things you do that show you're a quality performer. Here are four examples to give you the idea:

1. **Sign those phone messages.** Nothing is more frustrating than to need more information about a phone message on your desk and not know who it is from. Sign all messages you leave.

2. **Be a quality advocate.** The next time you witness an example of great service or outstanding quality, call and tell the person responsible how impressed you are. People are so used to getting only complaint calls that your positive message will bowl them over.

3. **Know your products.** No matter what position you hold with your company, you should know what your products or services do. The best way to gain this knowledge is to use them yourself. Ask your product manager for a hands-on demonstration or trial use so you can get firsthand knowledge.

4. **Be accountable.** No matter how careful you are, mistakes can happen. If they do, maintain your integrity by being accountable. Don't say, "Well, you misunderstood me." Instead say, "I'm sorry, I guess I didn't make myself clear."

QUALITIES IN ACTION

It takes a little practice to develop any personal quality. Try the exercise on the following page to get a head start.

First, return to page 54 at the beginning of this session and take a look at the list you made in the exercise **What Is Quality Made Of?** Select any five of those qualities you listed. (There are additional qualities in the **Answers Section** at the end of this session. You may select five of those if you prefer, or mix and match between your list and the **Answers Section** list.)

After each quality you have chosen, write down one action you can take that would demonstrate this quality. Use the actions discussed in **Four Quick Tips For Showing Your Qualities** as examples.

For instance, if the quality you choose is "dependability," your action might be "makes a point of returning all phone calls promptly."

Quality #1 _____

Action _____

_____

_____

_____

Quality #2 _____

Action _____

_____

_____

_____

Quality #3 _____

Action _____

_____

_____

_____

Quality #4 _____

Action _____

_____

_____

_____

Quality #5 _____

Action _____

_____

_____

_____

CASE STUDY #2:
A QUALITY PROPOSAL

Catherine had always prided herself on being a quality performer. Her work had been at a consistently high level over the last several years and had produced positive results. She knew she was being seriously considered for a major promotion.

Catherine was part of a work team that consisted of eight people. Each one of them took turns acting as the spokesperson for the group. It was Catherine's turn. The proposal for which she was to speak was somewhat unconventional. Catherine reviewed the proposal and realized it made perfect sense. It was exactly the type of "quality" idea she had pursued.

The problem, Catherine knew, was the company. In a huge organization loaded down with structural rules and procedures, there was simply no way the top managers would consider it. It would be deemed too "radical," and Catherine could well imagine their incredulous reaction. Her new division manager in particular — with whom Catherine did not have a very good relationship — would reject the idea out of hand. Presenting it would be a waste of time and could very well damage her chance for advancement. Despite her success, she knew she was thought of as a "free thinker" and not trusted by some to carry out the company's policies. She didn't want to jeopardize her chances of a promotion, but at the same time she felt she had a responsibility to her team to make a concerted effort to get the plan approved.

What should Catherine do? What would you do?

_____

_____

_____

_____

_____

_____

Would you give the presentation of the plan an all-out effort or simply place it before your boss, knowing it would be rejected? Would you go around your immediate boss to someone higher up in the company?

_____

_____

_____

_____

_____

_____

How would you counter the inevitable objections to the plan? Objections such as "It's completely against company policy" and "If we did this for your group, we'd have to do it for everyone in the company."

_____

_____

_____

_____

_____

_____

WHAT IS QUALITY MADE OF?

Here are some of the qualities that make for a quality performer:

1. Dependability

2. Accountability

3. Commitment

4. Knowledge

5. Confidence

6. Ability

7. Good communication skills

8. Personality

DO YOU REMEMBER?

Can you recall **The 3 Guiding Principles to Personal Quality**? Write them here.

1. _____

2. _____

3. _____

Based on what you've learned in Session 4, rate yourself again on the following statements. When you are finished, compare your total score with the one you earned at the beginning of this session.

WEAK	AVERAGE	STRONG
1–4 points	5–7 points	8–10 points

I have an ongoing commitment always to do quality work.   _____

I am good at paying attention to the everyday mundane tasks.   _____

I always take responsibility for whatever I do.   _____

I can perform consistently at a high level.   _____

I am conscious of the need for quality within the company.   _____

I have a thorough knowledge of company products and services.   _____

I believe in being accountable for whatever I do, including mistakes.   _____

I have confidence in my own abilities.   _____

I communicate clearly; I am rarely misunderstood or asked to reexplain.   _____

I am personable; co-workers and clients like to work with me.   _____

TOTAL RATING   _____

WEAK	FAIR	GOOD	STRONG
Under 40	41–55	56–74	75–100

ACTION PLAN

Many of the skills explained in this chapter are interrelated, and building from your strengths is a good place to start improving your overall abilities. But you can't afford to overlook your weaknesses either. List below your three best scores (your strengths) and your three lowest scores (your weaknesses) from the ratings on the previous page.

STRENGTHS

1. _____
2. _____
3. _____

WEAKNESSES

1. _____
2. _____
3. _____

Comparing the two lists, can you see any ways in which you can use your strengths to improve your weaknesses? If so, write them down.

_____

_____

_____

Now reexamine your three biggest weaknesses. It's best to work on them one at a time, so list them in this order: Start with the one you think will be easiest to improve upon, followed by a more difficult one, then the most difficult one.

Next to each, set a timetable for concentrating on them (one week, two weeks, and so on).

WEAKNESSES

1. _____
2. _____
3. _____

TIMETABLE FOR WORKING ON IMPROVEMENT

1. _____
2. _____
3. _____

Using the ideas and information from this session, list at least one technique you can practice to improve each weakness. Also add any ideas of your own.

1. _____
2. _____
3. _____

S U M M A R Y

Responsibility ... commitment ... consistency ... these and all of the other qualities that make up quality are the personal attributes that define a quality performer. But as we've shown, developing these attributes is only the first part of the quality equation. To be a true quality performer, you have to put them into action and to do so on a continuing basis. With the skills you have developed and the understanding you have gained from the exercises you have just worked through, you are now ready to do just that.

In Session 5, "Creating Quality Service," we'll look at that barometer of quality in action, namely customer service. We're going to concentrate on *creating* quality in service, and we'll give you a few insights that we believe are rather unique and that will also be new to you. That's quite a claim, in this era of emphasized customer service — but why don't you move ahead to Session 5 now and see if we aren't right?

CREATING QUALITY SERVICE

I N T R O D U C T I O N

Prior to the early 1980s, most literature about quality focused on the physical product. "Service" quality was a by-product of marketing, something that either helped a customer choose a product or use it later. Service was something extra — something having to do with things such as payment terms, directions for use, guarantees, repairs, maintenance, and other "nonhuman" issues.

Today, you can page through scores of books about quality and virtually all of them define quality in terms of customers and customer satisfaction. And that makes sense. A process, product, or service has no relevance without customers; everything that's done in an organization is done for the customer.

Attracting, serving, and retaining customers is the ultimate purpose of any company. Without a customer focus, a commitment to quality is meaningless.

Our focus in this fifth and final session will be on how to create quality service. After the opening **Pre-Session Skill Level Assessment**, we'll begin with a quick look at some work habits you can develop to ensure that you provide that all-important quality in servicing your customers. It's called **Four Easy Steps to Creating Quality.**

Quality is in the eye of the beholder; it's the customer who is the ultimate judge of the quality of your service. How can you know what those customers are thinking? That's the subject of the next feature, **How to Cash In on Customer Feedback**.

There are two exercises in this feature. **Active Feedback,** which will show you how to get the information you need, and **Passive Feedback,** in which you'll discover a few ways to tell when the customer is unhappy even when the customer isn't telling.

Case Study #l: A Chill in the Meeting will give you chance to apply those newly found skills in the midst of a particularly tricky situation.

Speaking of feedback, the next item will give you the opportunity to learn something about yourself. How good are you with people? Do people react well to you ... or are they being something less than flattering behind your back? Regardless of what you think, it's their opinion that matters. Find out how good you are with people by taking the quiz **People Skills Essential to Quality Service.**

Is quality a function of time? That's a question we'll address in **Do You Have to Compromise Quality for Speed?** Given the chronic shortage of time in today's business world, it's an especially important topic. Here are a few pointers for getting that task done within the boss' impossible deadline ... and for getting it done in quality fashion.

Case Study #2: Fast but Good will help you to develop some of your own strategies for working quickly but well; strategies you can add to the tips we'll be mentioning.

The session winds to a conclusion with some inspiring advice to help you through the years as you pursue your career path — **A Credo to Work (and Live) By.**

And it's pure quality.

In addition we will have our final **Answers Section, Do You Remember? pop quiz, Post-Session Skill Level Assessment**, and **Action Plan**.

Now, here's Session 5, "Creating Quality Service."

Using the following scale, rate your own skills as they relate to the following statements.

WEAK	AVERAGE	STRONG
1–4 points	5–7 points	8–10 points

I have steps or set procedures that increase quality performance. _____

I aggressively seek out feedback from customers. _____

I can work to a tight deadline without sacrificing quality. _____

I work at developing effective "people skills." _____

I can recognize unspoken signs of customer dissatisfaction. _____

I am good at organizing my workload. _____

I can recognize what's important and what isn't when under a deadline. _____

I always keep clients or customers up-to-date on changes. _____

I can maintain concentration under pressure. _____

I am effective at eliciting feedback and responding to it. _____

TOTAL RATING _____

WEAK	FAIR	GOOD	STRONG
Under 40	41–55	56–74	75–100

Any score under 55 means there is room for improvement. A score between 56 and 74 means you are doing well but can do better. Any score over 75 means it is just a matter of building on your strengths.

You can have every attribute of personal quality, but it may mean little if you do not translate it into customer service. As a professional, you play a pivotal role in your company's commitment to quality and excellence. You are on the front line, dealing with the client. You report the bad — as well as the good — to the people who can change or improve your product or service.

Here are four easy things you can do to help your firm, and yourself, achieve better quality in both materials and services:

1. **Listen to clients.** Spend the time to discover your clients' wants, desires, frustrations, and successes. Know how they use your products or services in specific detail. Knowing them better will help you serve them better.

2. **Ask questions.** Don't let a quietly simmering problem boil over from lack of attention. Learn to ask your clients effective questions about the performance of your products and services. Write down what they tell you.

3. **Report findings.** Immediately and completely share the information about your clients with those who can bring about change. A small alteration, such as changing a service schedule or modifying product design, can vastly improve what you offer to customers. It might even make the difference between buying from you or a competitor.

4. **Notify clients.** If your company effects a change (and policy permits) call the client back to let him or her know what's been done. Not only will your customer know you've really listened, but he or she will also have a sense of partnership with you, your company, and its quality and excellence. If your client realizes that your firm constantly strives to improve, he or she will keep coming back — and everyone benefits. But you can achieve this only through effective, regular communications with your clients and management.

Memorize these four easy steps to creating quality. Integrate them into your daily performance at work and make them a part of your personal "quality" attitude.

How are you doing? Are you increasing your knowledge, improving your personal image, advancing your career? Or are you spinning your wheels? According to Plato, "The life that is unexamined is not worth living." How true! Self-assessment is the key to self-improvement.

If you are employed in sales or as a customer service representative, self-assessment from a career and job standpoint is inextricably tied to one critical question: How do your customers feel about the products and services they are getting? Self-assessment is well and good, but unless it matches your customers' assessment, you may be falling short of the mark.

How can you be certain you're not? The best way is to obtain and cash in on customer feedback. This feedback can be communicated in either active or passive fashion, and it's really not too difficult, as the next two exercises will show.

Exercise: Active Feedback

To pursue feedback actively, it's simply a matter of questioning the customer directly. Using your own business or service as an example, write down four questions you might ask one of your customers to elicit feedback:

1. _____

2. _____

3. _____

4. _____

If you're having trouble, take a look at the suggested questions listed in the **Answers Section** on page 77. Those are, of necessity, of a general nature but can help you get a better fix on the types of questions to ask. If you have looked at them before writing your own answers, try again — this time framing more specific questions geared to your own situation.

Exercise: Passive Feedback

Passive feedback is the kind that comes to you for free, and it can be equally, if not more, enlightening. A customer complaint, for example, can be a valuable input for service and sales personnel — an indication that something is amiss and needs attention.

Not all customers readily voice their complaints, and this may cause the problem to fester. Customers who keep their complaints to themselves are well on the way to becoming ex-customers. You'll have to keep your eyes and ears open to detect passive feedback from this type of customer. But there are at least three telltale signs — and they all involve a change in the customer's behavior.

Write examples of changes in a customer's behavior that may mean he or she is sending you negative passive feedback:

1. _____

2. _____

3. _____

When you detect negative passive feedback, switch to an action mode and use the active means to uncover the reasons for the customer's discontent. Then you can take the necessary steps to correct the problem and cash in on the customer's feedback.

The answers to this exercise are in the **Answers Section** on page 77. But don't look there yet! If you had trouble coming up with answers for the exercise, the following case study will give you some clues.

CASE STUDY #1:
A CHILL IN THE MEETING

Sarah was vaguely troubled and couldn't decide if her concerns were real or if she was just being paranoid.

She and her customer Brenda had just concluded a brief but efficient meeting. There had been a few minor points to iron out but everything had gone smoothly. Except ….

Brenda had not seemed quite like her normal self. Sarah had worked with Brenda for more than a year now, and usually there was an easygoing camaraderie between the two of them. But today Brenda had seemed somewhat distracted. Was she under pressure at work for some reason Sarah was unaware of? Was she having a personal problem?

Sarah didn't know, and it was none of her business anyway. She tried to push the unease from her mind, but it kept gnawing at her. Brenda had seemed a bit more formal and businesslike than usual. A bit more aloof. And thinking on it some more, Sarah realized that Brenda's calls to her had become less frequent over the past month. Or was she imagining that, too?

And today ... Sarah had a special discount offer to show Brenda at the end of their meeting. It was the type of thing Brenda was usually quite interested in. But Brenda had only listened politely and taken a copy of the details, saying she'd get back to Sarah on it. Then she had hurried out of the meeting room and returned to her office. Was Sarah simply being paranoid? Or was there a darker reason for her discontent?

What should Sarah do? What would you do?

_____

_____

_____

_____

_____

_____

People Skills Essential to Quality Service

Dealing with customers, internal or external, is a vital and unavoidable part of any job. The skills you will need to succeed fall into two categories: product/service knowledge and "people skills." A complete understanding of your company's products and services can be acquired by studying and asking questions. People skills are somewhat less easily obtained. The following questions will help you determine what people skills you need. Answer each question **YES** or **NO**:

1. Do you expect the best from people? _____

2. Can you remember other people's names? _____

3. When someone is talking, can you devote your full attention to what is being said? _____

4. Can you accept others' views, decisions, and behaviors even if they are contrary to your own? _____

5. Are you lavish with praise and stingy with criticism? _____

6. Do you sincerely sympathize with others' troubles and take pleasure in their successes? _____

7. Do you look people directly in the eye? _____

8. Are you willing to admit your mistakes and correct them? _____

9. When talking to an angry or hostile person, can you avoid getting upset? _____

10. Do you make it a point never to get a cheap laugh at the expense of others? _____

YOUR PEOPLE SKILLS: If you had seven or more **YES** responses, your people skills are in good shape. If you scored lower, remember that the kind of skills you need to work well with customers goes far beyond being polite and knowing when to smile. Customer service involves conflict resolution, negotiation, psychology, temper control, nonverbal interpretation, and, yes, a little mind-reading. But don't let all that intimidate you. If you genuinely like people and are sincerely proud of the product or service your organization provides, you should find customer service very rewarding.

DO YOU HAVE TO COMPROMISE QUALITY FOR SPEED?

Quality is always great to strive for, but let's be realistic. There are times when the boss "needs it done yesterday." Do you have to compromise quality for speed? Obviously, the more time you have to work on something the better the final product will be. Or will it? There is such a thing as being too much of a perfectionist. Crossing every last "t" and dotting every last "i" can use up far more time than it's worth.

Your boss no doubt appreciates quality work. But even a great job doesn't do anyone any good if it isn't completed in time. And that's the key. Time. Your boss isn't asking you to sacrifice quality; just to do the job *as well as you can within the time frame.*

What steps can you take to blend speed with quality? We do have a few tips — they're listed in the **Answers Section** on pages 77 and 78 — but this time we're going to ask what you think first. Read the following case study and list the steps you would take to solve the problem.

CASE STUDY #2: FAST BUT GOOD

John's boss burst into his office and dropped the two-inch-thick file of computer printouts on his desk. "Quarterly sales figures," he said. "I need a region-by-region breakdown and an analysis."

John's company was a national retailer, and his boss wanted a determination of which products — by region — were not selling well. "The computer can do some of it for you," John's boss said, "but it can't do the analysis. It can't tell us *why* some of our merchandise is on the downswing. That's your job. Look for patterns and if you can identify them, make some recommendations."

It was a huge job and time was very short. John's boss needed the analysis to present to the executive committee in three days. He told John that he had chosen John for the project because he knew how meticulous and methodical John was — even if John often took too much time to complete his assignments. "This time I need it fast but good," John's boss said. "I know you can do it."

Well then, John thought after his boss left, he'd just have to apply his slow methodical approach toward working more quickly. He began writing down a list of guidelines for himself to complete the project on time — and still do a quality job — before he started working on the task. He came up with six of them.

Imagine that you're in John's position. What guidelines can you think of to speed the work along without sacrificing its quality? Write them in the following space. John's guidelines are in the **Answers Section** on page 77 and 78. After you've written down your list, compare it with John's.

1. _____

2. _____

3. _____

4. _____

5. _____

6. _____

A CREDO TO WORK (AND LIVE) BY

Finally, some words of wisdom to conclude this workbook. No, there won't be a quiz on them later. But you might want to take them to heart just the same.

- **Believe in yourself completely.** Have faith in your ability to do anything you set out to do.

- **Believe in what you are doing.** Know that you have the ability to help others find solutions to their problems.

- **See yourself as successful.** Virtually everyone has some redeeming qualities. Develop a self-image that includes personal success.

- **Appreciate your assets.** Demonstrate in appearance, manner, voice, and spirit that you have value to your company.

- **Recognize the importance and value of others.** Strive to enhance the quality of life for everyone you touch; remember, they ultimately contribute to your own quality of life.

- **Like yourself.** The more you like yourself, the more generous you'll be toward others.

- **Look at your problems as opportunities.** Welcome change and the challenges you face. They give you a chance to stretch your abilities.

- **Plan your work well; then work your plans.** Live by your own agenda. When flying through each day, sit in the pilot's seat instead of in the passenger section.

- **Allow yourself the luxury of enthusiasm.** It can make or break even the best-laid plans.

A C T I V E   F E E D B A C K

Examples of questions you can ask the customer include the following:

1. Was the problem resolved to your complete satisfaction?

2. Do you have any complaints about the product or service?

3. Is there anything about the transaction you would like to clarify?

4. Do you have any reservations about the way it was handled?

P A S S I V E   F E E D B A C K

Three telltale signs or changes in behavior include the following:

1. An unaccustomed coolness or aloofness on the customer's part.

2. A decline in orders or calls.

3. A lack of interest in special offers or new products, often reflected in the look in the customer's eyes or the sound of his or her voice.

C A S E   S T U D Y   # 2 :
F A S T   B U T   G O O D

Here are the tips for working more quickly without sacrificing quality that John wrote down:

1. **Determine what is important and what isn't.** Your work time is limited and you are probably under a tight deadline. Try to define clearly what your priorities are.

2. **Outline a schedule.** Break the project down into steps; then outline an estimate for how long each step will take. If your calculations take you beyond the project deadline, review the steps to see which could be shortened or eliminated.

3. **Determine how many times you need to double-check details.** If you are checking and rechecking your work, you may be wasting valuable time.

4. **Organize your work.** If you don't take a systematic approach to work, you may mistakenly forget about something that you should have done and have to retrace your steps.

5. **Increase your concentration.** One of the reasons you feel you need to check and recheck your work may be because you are not concentrating enough. Try to tune out distractions and focus on what you are doing.

6. **Write it down.** If you have a hard time remaining on a specific schedule, at the start of each day, write down what you need to accomplish. List priorities that must get done for the production process to flow smoothly. This will help keep you and your department on track.

DO YOU REMEMBER?

Can you recall the **Four Easy Steps to Creating Quality** from this session? List them here:

1. _____

2. _____

3. _____

4. _____

Based on what you've learned in Session 5, rate yourself again on the following statements. When you are finished, compare your total score with the one you earned at the beginning of this session:

WEAK	AVERAGE	STRONG
1–4 points	5–7 points	8–10 points

I have steps or set procedures that increase quality performance. _____

I aggressively seek out feedback from customers. _____

I can work to a tight deadline without sacrificing quality. _____

I work at developing effective "people skills." _____

I can recognize unspoken signs of customer dissatisfaction. _____

I am good at organizing my workload. _____

I can recognize what's important and what isn't when under a deadline. _____

I always keep clients or customers up-to-date on changes. _____

I can maintain concentration under pressure. _____

I am effective at eliciting feedback and responding to it. _____

TOTAL RATING _____

WEAK	FAIR	GOOD	STRONG
Under 40	41–55	56–74	75–100

A C T I O N   P L A N

Many of the skills explained in this chapter are interrelated, and building from your strengths is a good place to start improving your overall abilities. But you can't afford to overlook your weaknesses either. List your three best scores (your strengths) and your three lowest scores (your weaknesses) from the ratings on the previous page:

STRENGTHS

1. _____

2. _____

3. _____

WEAKNESSES

1. _____

2. _____

3. _____

Comparing the two lists, can you see any ways in which you can use your strengths to improve your weaknesses? If so, write them down.

_____

_____

_____

Now reexamine your three biggest weaknesses. It's best to work on them one at a time, so list them in this order: Start with the one you think will be easiest to improve upon, followed by a more difficult one, then the most difficult one.

Next to each, set a timetable for concentrating on them (one week, two weeks, and so on):

WEAKNESSES

1. _____

2. _____

3. _____

TIMETABLE FOR WORKING ON IMPROVEMENT

1. _____

2. _____

3. _____

Using the ideas and information from this session, list at least one technique you can practice to improve each weakness. Also add any ideas of your own.

1. _____

2. _____

3. _____

S U M M A R Y

If there's a single most important thing to remember about personal quality performance, it is that it's a perception ... a perception that reflects the reality. It's what the customer perceives in you that tells whether you're performing on a "quality" level. And, as we've just seen, that perception is most readily found in the area of your customer service.

In your efforts to enhance your quality performance, feedback is vital. So is the ability to work under pressure, and to work quickly but well. So too, for that matter, are all of the other points and skills we've covered, not only in Session 5 but in this entire workbook.

We hope you take these skills, attitudes, and perceptions to heart and that you put them to effective use. We know you'll find them helpful in your continuing search for quality, both in your work and in yourself. And we wish you the best of continued success in your career.